Presented To:

____

By:

____

Date:

____

55 Tough Tongue Twisters

"A Word Fitly Spoken Is Like Apples of Gold in Settings Of Silver" (King Solomon).

J.J. Turner, Ph.D.

SOLUTIONS 2.0

WHAT IS A TONGUE TWISTER?

Tongue-twister (noun): A sequence of words or sounds typically of an alliterative kind, that are different to pronounce quickly and correctly, as, for example: <u>tie twine to three tree twigs</u>

SPEAKING CLEARLY

Words need to be understood
Before they can be obeyed;
So please dear speaker
Pronounce clearly what you say.

Words are life and death instruments
So they must not be cut or hacked;
So please enunciate them clearly
So we'll both be on the same track.

I encourage you to use Tongue Twisters
To correct any hacking ways;
They'll help you become more efficient
As listener hear what you have to say.

So don't be a word hacker
Remember King Solomon said it best;
A word clearly and distinctly spoken
Will pass the "I get it" test.

(J.J. Turner, Ph.D. © 2020)

INTRODUCTION

At one time or another—sooner or later—we all have come across words such as *Massachusetts (Mas-sa-chu-setts),* which we found difficult to pronounce or enunciate clearly or properly.

Many speeches with great and needed content are lost because the speaker didn't pronounce words correctly or cut them off without clear enunciation.

When I was in the 5th grade, Mrs. Merchant made what I thought was a big deal out of pronouncing and enunciating words correctly. She also stressed that the only place "ain't" should crawl out of was an "ant hill" not a human mouth.

I still remember some of the key tongue twisters I learned in school, which were designed to help us southern boys do a better job with the King's English. Here are a few of those tongue twisters:

- ✓ *Peter Piper picked a pack of pickled peppers. How many picked peppers did Peter Piper pick?*

- ✓ *She sells seashells down by the seashore. Down by the seashore she sells seashells.*

- ✓ *Around the rugged rock the ragged rascal ran. The ragged rascal ran around the rugged rock.*

- ✓ *I scream, you scream, we all scream for ice cream; for ice cream we all scream.*

- ✓ *Fuzzy Wuzzy was a bear. Fuzzy Wuzzy had no hair. Fuzzy Wuzzy was fuzzy, was he?*

- ✓ *How can a clam cram in a cream can?*
- ✓ *Can you can a can as a canner can can a can?*

- ✓ I saw Susie sitting in a shoe shine shop, shining shines on shoes.

- ✓ I thought a thought, but the thought I thought wasn't the thought I thought.

Tongue twisters are fun exercises to improve pronunciation in English. They also help improve accents by using alliteration, which is the repeating of one sound.

Tongue twister aren't only for children, but also for adults such as public speakers, actors, lawyers, ministers, teachers, and politicians who want to be clearly understood by making sure each word is pronounced and enunciate clearly.

About 30 years ago I started writing tongue twisters for my nephew, Brandon. It was a fun project we shared. I compiled a few of them in a booklet and presented them as a gift. I have recently found those original twisters, as well as a manuscript of a few additional tongue twisters.

You hold in your hand the tongue twister I wrote back then as well as few new ones written recently.

To maximize the benefits and fun from these tongue twisters I offer these suggestions:

1. Meet with a group of friends and share them. It is a fun exercise.
2. Once you have mastered saying a twister once, try to say it twice or three more times as rapidly as possible. Speed it the key to success.
3. Use them as private exercises to improve your pronouncing and enunciating words.
4. Memorize some and use them in waiting times or moments when you need to divert your thinking.

King Solomon said, *"There is nothing new under the sun."* As far as I can remember I haven't read these tongue twisters anywhere else. That's doesn't mean that I haven't on a subconscious level stored words and phrases from other twisters. All I can say

is "Thank you" for the twister if it was original with you.

I hope you enjoy these few tongue twisters.
I encourage you to write your own.

TONGUE TWISTERS

55 TONGUE TWISTERS

Dimple Dolly Dimpler dove down dangerously deep; down dangerously deep Dimple Dolly Dimpler dove.

Adam Apple admittedly added additional answers annually; additional answers were annually added admittedly by Adam Apple.

Dull Dug Dugan dug deep ditches daily, deep ditches daily dull Dug Dugan dug.

Tree tumbling Tommy tumbled through tall trees; through tall trees tumbling Tommy tumbled.

Allen Alta added additives actively; additives were actively added by Allen Alta.

Cool crude cruisers crushed candy; candy was crushed by cool cruisers candidly.

Wilber Webb was a weather web watcher;
A weather web watchers was Wilber Webb.

Red Reese Reed rotated real rubber rims;
Real rubber rims Red Reese Reed rotated.

Billy Bud brilliantly blocked batted balls,
Batted balls were brilliantly blocked by Billy
Bud.

Pink pigs portly pranced proudly in parades;
proudly in parades pink portly pigs pranced.

Sam Shore shared soaring scoring scrolls;
Soaring scoring scrolls Sam Shore shared.

Bill boiled big broccoli butter basted;
Butter basted broccoli Bill boiled hastily.

Charles choked on a cold coke; on a cold
coke Charles choked.

Rough road rogue roaches race rodents;
Rodents race rough rogue roaches.

Billy Blade braded Betty Blazer's hair; Betty
Blazer's hair Billy Blade braded.

Papa proudly posted positive posters;
Positive posters Papa proudly posted.

Easter eats easily the essence of each meal;
the essence of each meal Easter easily eats.

Eddie edits eight editions eighty time;

Eighty times Eddie edits eight editions.

Fred fed fresh fish; fresh fish Fred Fed.

Denise denied fleas on her fleece; fleas were denied by Denise of her fleece.

Irate Irene invites innocent Ivan inside; innocent Ivan is invited inside by Irene.

Joking Joe jolted jolly Joey; Jolly Joey jolted joking Joe.

Kind Kyle kidded Kitty Killian; Kitty Killian kind Kyle kidded.

Little leaping Lee leaped leaking ditches; leaking ditches were leaped by little leaping Lee.

Molly Mole mowed more mulch; more mulch Molly Mole mowed.

Noble Nan's nanny needed nine nails; nine nails noble Nan's nanny needed.

Only old Opal opened all her options;
All her options were opened by old Opal.

Piker Peter peaked at Peter peeper; Peter peeper peeked at piker Peter.

Quick Quincy quit quickly quarreling; quickly Quick Quincy quit quarreling.

Ulysses' uncle's union unionized unicorns; unicorns were unionized by Ulysses' uncle.

Vic viciously vented his vexed vibrations; vexed vibration Vic viciously vented.

While waiting wales wallowed wildly, Wally watched while waiting wales wallowed.

East easement exits existed easterly; exits existed on easterly east easement.

Turner tongue twisters twist the tongue; the tongue is twisted by Turner tongue twisters.

Yellow yokes yielding to yelling yokels; yokels yielding to yellow yokes yelling.

Cowardly cow crawled crouching; crouching the cowardly cow crawled.

Freddie's fangs faintly fell foul; faintly Freddie's foul fangs fell.

Sierra Sarah sings sad slow songs; sad slow songs sings Sierra Sarah.

Barry bear barely buried barriers; barely buried berries Barry bear buried.

French friends find frolic fun; frolic fun finds French friends friendly.

Congo cargo carried cartooned cars; cartooned cars Congo cargo carried.

Flip Flipper flipped five fish; five fish Flip Flipper flipped.

Rained rain ran running roughly downhill; downhill rained rain ran downhill roughly.

Sid Sunday sips six sundaes slowly; six sundaes are sipped slowly by Sid Sunday.

Thirty tired turtles taking turns turning; taking turns thirty tired turtles turn.

Whipping Willie had a willow whip; a willow whip whipping Willie had.

Piled pillared pyramid pillows are piled; pyramid pillars are piled pillows.

Royal Ray raised rated raisins, rated raisins were raised by Royal Ray.

Wound up Wiley Woody would work wood; wood would Wiley Woody work.

Strict Stanley staggered straightly when sedated; when sedated Strict Stanley staggered straightly.

Fred Friday fried five fresh fish on Friday, Friday fresh fish were friend by Fred Friday.

Squire squirrel squandered seven seeds secretly; secretly Squire Squirrel squandered seven seeds.

The big black bull died bellowing,
Bellowing the big black bull died.

Sarah sent five shiny cents,
Five shiny cents Sarah sent.

The night was dangerously dark,
Dark was the dangerous night.

Ned neatly nailed nine new nails,
Nine new nails Ned neatly nailed.

Hal heard the Owl howling,
The howling Owl was heard by Hal.

Daily Dave dated Debra,
Debra dated Dave daily.

Sister switched the six stiches,
The six stiches were switched by sister.

Little Billy fiddled with his fiddle,
On his fiddle little Billy fiddled.

Joe jumped jumping jacks with Joey,
Joey jumped jumping jacks with Joe.

Fred fried five fifty-five fish,
fifty-five fish Fred fried.

Thirty tricky tongue twisters
Were twisted on Tom's tongue.

Tired tall trembling Tim
Climbed three trembling
Tall trees three times.

Where were whirlwinds whirling
When wild whirlwinds weren't whirling?

For additional materials by the author please visit his website:

www.jeremiahinstitute.com